Thomas Spence

Useful and Practical Hints for the Settler on Canadian Prairie Lands

Thomas Spence

Useful and Practical Hints for the Settler on Canadian Prairie Lands

ISBN/EAN: 9783744759854

Printed in Europe, USA, Canada, Australia, Japan

Cover: Foto ©Andreas Hilbeck / pixelio.de

More available books at **www.hansebooks.com**

SECOND EDITION, REVISED AND CORRECTED.

USEFUL AND PRACTICAL HINTS FOR THE SETTLER

ON

CANADIAN PRAIRIE LANDS

AND FOR THE

GUIDANCE OF INTENDING BRITISH EMIGRANTS

TO

Manitoba and the North-West of Canada.

WITH FACTS

REGARDING THE SOIL, CLIMATE, PRODUCTS, ETC., AND THE SUPERIOR
ATTRACTIONS AND ADVANTAGES POSSESSED, IN COMPARISON
WITH THE WESTERN PRAIRIE STATES OF AMERICA.

BY

THOMAS SPENCE,
CLERK OF THE LEGISLATIVE ASSEMBLY OF MANITOBA.

Second Edition, Revised and Corrected.

1882.

PREFACE.

This is the fifth pamphlet published by the writer on the resources of the great North-West of the Dominion of Canada. His first issue for the information of the outside world, which appeared in June, 1871, was compiled with much care, labour, and difficulty, he is proud to say, has ever since been extensively used as an authority by the Press, not only of Canada and Great Britain, but the United States, and also received the commendation of all the public men of the country; it, and later editions covering a wider field, remain standard books of reference on the subject. For over ten years he has devoted himself and his pen to the task of making the unsurpassed resources of the vast Prairie Lands of Canada, familiar to the people of Great Britain, as the nearest and best field for the investment of their labour and surplus means. That he has not laboured wholly without reward, the liberal patronage and gratuitous distribution by the Dominion Government of several editions on both sides of the Atlantic, and the unprecedented flow of immigration as the result, affords the truest indication.

Since his first publication appeared, a magical transformation has taken place—from a country then peopled by only Indians, natives, fur traders, and a few of an adventurous class, clustering about the chief settlement of the Red River, to a Province filled with churches and school houses, a flourishing city as the capital and gateway, with a population of over 12,000, and rapidly increasing, the country dotted with thriving villages, and hundreds of miles of the Canadian Pacific Railway completed and running, giving us direct connection with the east, and stretching far over our fertile and beautiful Prairies to the west, ere long to span the continent from ocean to ocean, when with her elevators filled with wheat, furnishing the world's markets with flour, her influence will be felt from England to Russia.

In this, as in the previous publications, there has been no attempt to depict in glowing colours the resources of the country, beyond the warrant of facts.

The subjoined few of the many opinions of the Press, are submitted to the intending emigrant, that entire confidence may be reposed in the information contained in this work, and the author respectfully bespeaks for it a careful and attentive perusal, by all who are desirous of procuring homes and improving their condition, by settling in a country with home institutions, protected by the same flag, and already renowned for BEAUTY, FERTILITY, HEALTH AND PROSPERITY.

THOS. SPENCE.

St. Boniface, Manitoba, Jan., 1882.

4

OPINIONS OF THE PRESS.

FROM THE CHICAGO INTER-OCEAN.

Mr. Spence has shown himself an admirable special pleader on behalf of that vast portion of Canada, and we must admit, although he does draw comparisons somewhat unfavorable to the Western States and Territories of the Union, that he is ready, with chapter and verse, for every fact which he puts forth. Canada's maxim now is: Build railways, and the country will soon be settled. She is now building her Canadian Pacific Railway, which will run for a thousand miles through that rich and beautiful country. This is a very shrewd dodge upon the part of our slow, but sure, neighbors across the line, and we do not doubt that, by the dissemination of such phamphlets as this of Mr. Spence, the hopes of the projectors will, in process of time, be realized. He goes minutely into a description of the entire fertile country, and, besides, gives a vast amount of information valuable and necessary for intending emigrants.—*Chicago Inter-Ocean, June 16, 1877.*

MANITOBA AND THE NORTH-WEST—ITS RESOURCES, &c., &c.

BY THOMAS SPENCE.

The author throws himself heartily into his subject, and, from his several years residence in the North-West and general information, has qualified himself to handle it effectively. All who take an interest in our new region should procure and study it. We can endorse the compliment paid to it by the late Lieutenant-Governor, Mr. Archibald, as follows:

"I have read Mr. Spence's pamphlet entitled 'Manitoba and the North-West,' with much interest. It draws the comparison with much force and description, and altogether the pamphlet is a valuable contribution on the subject of the North-West, and of particular value to the intending emigrant."—*Ottawa Times, 1874.*

MANITOBA AND ITS RESOURCES, &C., &C.

This, with the result of personal experience and observation, is by far the most valuable publication upon Manitoba, and most practical, as well as the most reliable means of conveying information for the guidance of the immigrant. It has received the highest encomiums from the late Sir George Cartier and others.—*Ottawa Free Press, May, 1874.*

THE PRAIRIE LANDS OF CANADA.

BY THOMAS SPENCE, Clerk Legislative Assembly of Manitoba.

"The Prairie Lands of Canada."—A pamphlet with this title, from the pen of Mr. Thomas Spence, Clerk of the Legislative Assembly, Manitoba, will shortly be issued. The known ability of this gentleman for compiling and making attractive the facts, which a long residence in our West and keen powers of observation present to him, are a guarantee that this work will be as valuable and popular as all his former efforts in the same direction have been. Since the publication of "Manitoba and its Resources," by Mr. Spence, the circumstances of the establishment of a Government in the great uncircumscribed North-West, and the increasing activities of emigration ever Westward, have enlarged the field of observation for writers on the subject, and the present work proves how fully capable the author is of doing justice to the task. The former treatise referred to received the commendation of all the public men of the country, as the best book that had appeared on the subject, and became the accepted book of reference on Manitoba with the public. We are confident that the success of the present work will ever outrun that of the earlier, and we predict that it must become the standard book of reference on the subject. Every one who has anything of national spirit should have a copy.—*Montreal Gazette.*

CONTENTS.

INTRODUCTION.

The birth and growth of Manitoba and the North-West Territory, now filling out the tenth year of existence, as a part of the grand Confederation of Canada, is one of the most remarkable events which men in our day have the opportunity of seeing pass before them. From a large tract of country destitute of dwelling houses, of cultivated fields, of fixed inhabitants ; where Indians wandered over it, but did not leave a single trace of having made a home, or subdued the soil, of having changed the face of nature ; in the short space of ten years, a large area of this desolate waste has become the home of thousands of people, coming from each Canadian Province, the United States, Great Britain, Russia, Iceland, &c. Schools, churches mills and stores are met with almost everywhere in settlements of little over a year's growth, and opportunities for social intercourse are at the command of even those in the most sparsely settled neighborhoods. The hunting ground of the savage has been transformed into the home of the civilized and contented European ; and this growth of the past will be far transcended by the growth of the future. The inducements to-day offered by Manitoba and the North-West of Canada to immigrants cannot be surpassed, and are rarely equalled by any other country on the globe,—these comprise excellence of soil and water, agricultural and commercial advantages, and educational facilities ; and in addition to all these, cheap lands, and free homesteads of 160 acres, equally good, of which thousands of enterprising people are every year taking advantage, and the tenant farmer and man of small means daily attracted to the splendid opportunity here presented to acquire homes in such a productive country ; not a lease for any term of years, but a perpetual ownership, to transmit to his heirs, or he may sell it ; no landlord, no yearly rent to pay, nor are any church rates or tithings exacted. The settler's farm is his private domain, and his house is really his castle ; he becomes his own master for life, and leaves this precious legacy to his children.

It may be affirmed that whatever Manitoba is to-day, she owes solely to the inherent merits that God has given her, of soil, climate and production, developed by the energy, industry and perseverance of her people ; our success has been achieved without the phantom lures of gold or silver to blazon forth to the world, as was the case with California and Australia.

The jealousy of American Western Prairie States, and their railway landed interests, competing for immigration, circulating through their letters and papers false reports of our climate and soil, rendered necessary the writer's previous comparison and statements of facts as antidotes to these poisonous fables. But that day and era have passed. The new era has arrived of more general intelligence, and acquaintance more intimate and thorough with our commerce and our advantages of soil and climate. Our growth cannot be checked by human agency. Immigration to a prime wheat growing region can no more be prevented than to newly discovered gold regions.

The newspapers of Canada and Great Britain, and the reports of the delegates of tenant farmers, liberally invited by the Government of Canada to judge the merits of the country by personal visits, have contained glowing pictures of the wonderful fertility of our prairies. Instances have been published and scattered world-wide, showing the certainty of wealth, or at least competence to the farmer, in the Canadian North-West, with its gems of lakes, rivers, and fringes of timber; a region already cleared and fit for the husbandman, requiring only the turning of the sod and sowing of seed to convert a park into a farm. It is little wonder, then, that farming made so easy, and in a country so beautiful and attractive, should draw to it that rushing stream of immigrants which we daily witness, and that for years has been pouring into it.

The object of the present compilation is to afford later and more general information for the emigrant's guidance before leaving the old home for a new; and in addition, to furnish the most useful and practical advice to the settler commencing on his land. The utmost care has been observed throughout in the preparation of these pages, to avoid exaggeration in setting forth the inducements to immigrants. If mutual benefits are to flow from immigration, new settlers must not be attracted by representations which their future experience will not verify. *Cui Malo.*

USEFUL AND PRACTICAL HINTS.

WHO SHOULD EMIGRATE.

"The tillers of the soil" are the class who are most needed here, and who are most certain in achieving success by steady industry; in fact, any man, whatever his station in life may be, who is able and willing to work, and has any adaptability for agricultural pursuits, can, in the course of a few years, build up for himself and family a properous future and independence. Professional men and clerks should not come unless with means to take up land and commence the life of a farmer. Carpenters, blacksmiths, etc., with a little capital to start with, can, when not working on their land, secure employment in the nearest settlements, and do well. There is also a constant demand for female servants at good wages (who are certain soon to become their own mistress). Laborers who can handle a pick and shovel will meet with ready employment for some years to come, in consequence of the construction of the Canadian Pacific and other Railways, the wages averaging $1.50 and $1.75 per day, equal to six and seven shillings, stg. With prudence and economy he may soon save enough to start him on a free homestead of 160 acres, his own master.

The tenant farmer with some capital, who seeks to improve his condition by his experience, and desires larger and quicker returns for labor bestowed and capital invested, has unequalled advantages offered to him, and the ordinary immigrant with even a couple of hundred pounds to begin with, can start under very favorable circumstances on a free grant of land. Detailed particulars will be found under the appropriate headings.

GENERAL DIRECTIONS.

The intending settler in Manitoba is advised not to encumber himself with very heavy luggage unless it is absolutely necessary. Cumbrous and heavy articles of furniture, such as chairs, stoves, tables, etc., would probably cost as much in transport as they would be worth, and things of this sort can be obtained reasonably in Manitoba. But beds (unfilled), bedding, and clothing of all sorts should be taken. Agricultural implements (which should be of the kind adapted to the country) would be better purchased after arrival ; also tools, unless those belonging to special trades.

Sometimes, however, when a settler engages a car specially to take up his effects, he may find it convenient to put everything in, and there is very frequently an economy in this kind of arrangement.

Individual settlers are allowed 150 lbs. weight of luggage, and parties going together may arrange to have their luggage weighed together, and so have the whole averaged, but everything over 150 lbs. weight is charged, and this charge, in the case of freight of the kind referred to, is often found to be expensive.

The settler who goes by the lakes will find an officer of the Canadian Government at Duluth, Mr. W. C. B. Grahame. Mr. Grahame will assist him in bonding his luggage on entering the United States, and otherwise afford him every possible information. The Canadian Government has a large Settlers' Reception House at Duluth, at which immigrants may rest and refresh themselves.

Settlers going by way of the United States Railways must see that their personal luggage is examined by the U. S. Customs officers at Port Huron, after crossing the Canadian frontier at Sarnia, and previously that their heavy freight has been bonded.

At Emerson, an agent of the Canadian Goverment will be found, Mr. J. E. Tétu, and he will assist in discharging any bonds of immigrants' effects, and otherwise give information how to proceed.

At Winnipeg there is also a Canadian Immigration Agent, Mr. Wm. Hespeler, to whom immigrants may apply on arrival.

All intending settlers will obtain either from the Government Immigration Agents, or from the Land Officers, directions as to where to go and how to proceed to select land, if their point of destination is not previously determined. There are also Government Land Guides, who will direct parties of settlers to their particular localities.

All settlers are especially advised to look very closely after their luggage, and see that it is on the trains or steamboats with them, properly checked. Very great disappointment and loss have often occurred from neglect of this precaution. It is better for the immigrant not to proceed until he knows his luggage is on the train.

Settlers' effects, including their cattle in use, will be passed free through the Custom House, and any necessary bonding arrangements will be made, which will thus prevent any delay, inconvenience, or loss occurring. Each passenger, before his departure from the port in Great Britain, should be provided with address cards, and he should see that one is fastened to each of his pieces of luggage.

Immediately on the arrival of settlers in the Canadian North-West, the Dominion Government Agents will see them properly accommodated, and will give them every information to assist them in choosing a good locality to settle in.

For rates of passage, either ocean or inland, it is better to apply to the Agents of the steamships or the nearest Dominion Agent, who will give all information and directions.

The following are the officers of the Dominion of Canada in Great Britain :—

LONDON......SIR ALEXANDER T. GALT, G.C.M.G., &c., High Commissioner for the Dominion, 10 ʻʻictoria Chambers, London, S.W.

    MR. J. COLMER, Private Secretary, (Address as above).

LIVERPOOL.MR. JOHN DYKE, 15 Water Street.

GLASGOW ..MR. THOMAS GRAHAME, 40 Enoch Square.

BELFAST.....MR. CHARLES FOY, 29 Victoria Place.

DUBLIN ......MR. THOMAS CONNOLLY, Northumberland House.

The following are the Agents of the Canadian Government in Canada :

QUEBEC ......MR. L. STAFFORD, Point Levis, Quebec.

TORONTO ...MR. J. A. DONALDSON, Strachan Avenue, Toronto, Ontario.

OTTAWA......MR. W. J. WILLS, St. Lawrence and Ottawa Railway Station, Ottawa, Ontario.

MONTREAL.MR. J. J. DALEY, Bonaventure Street, Montreal, P.Q.

KINGSTON..MR. R. MACPHERSON, William Street, Kingston, Ontario.

HAMILTON .MR. JOHN SMITH, Great Western Railway Station, Hamilton, Ontario.

LONDON.. ...MR. A. G. SMYTH, London, Ontario.

HALIFAX....MR. E. CLAY, Halifax, Nova Scotia.

ST. JOHN......MR. S. GARDNER, St. John, New Brunswick.

WINNIPEG...MR. W. HESPELER, Winnipeg, Manitoba.

EMERSON ....MR. J. E. TÊTU, Railway Station, Emerson, Manitoba.

DULUTH.....MR. W. C. B. Grahame, Settlers' Reception House.

These officers will afford the fullest advice and protection. They should be immediately applied to on arrival. All complaints should be addressed to them. They will also furnish information as to Lands open for settlement in their respective Provinces and Districts, Farms for Sale, demand for employment, rates of wages, routes of travel, distances, expenses of conveyance ; and will receive and forward letters and remittances for Settlers, &c.

HOW TO COME—FARES, ROUTES, ETC.

The cost of conveyance from any part of Canada to Manitoba is exceedingly moderate, and the steamers from Great Britain are now so numerous, that the transport of a family from any part of the United Kingdom or from Canada to the great wheat growing region and cattle raising districts in the North West, cannot fairly be considered as a difficulty when the advantages offered are considered. A continuous line of railway now exists from Quebec and the different sea ports to Winnipeg and about two hundred miles west, and daily extending under rapid construction. An alternative route is offered by railway to Sarnia or Collingwood, and thence by first-class steamers to Prince Arthur's Landing and Duluth, at the head of Lake Superior. The time taken by the "lakes" is now about one day longer than by all rail, but in 1882, when the Canada Pacific will be opened from Prince Arthur's Landing, Thunder Bay, to Winnipeg, the trip by the "lakes" will be quicker than the fastest express trains of the all rail. Berths are provided for emigrant passengers, but they must bring their own bedding and provisions. Improvements have been added to the steamers, and the trip through the scenery of the lakes will give the traveller a good idea of the extent of the nationality among whom he has come to seek his home. At present the cost of carriage for each person (children reduced) is as follows: By rail all the way from Quebec *via* Chicago: For Emigrant or third-class (for emigrants from beyond the seas only), $21.64; or by the Lakes and Duluth, $16.64.

Cattle, goods, &c., are taken at reasonable charges by either route. Special arrangements have been made by the Grand Trunk Railway Company for emigrants going to Winnipeg in parties. To obtain the benefit of such arrangements, special application should be made in the case of each party. This may be done either directly to the head offices of the Company in London, 21 Old Bond Street, E.C., to the Company's offices in Montreal, or through any or the Dominion Government Emigration Agents. Through tickets for Winnipeg may be obtained in England, of the Railway or Steamship Companies, or their Agents.

WHEN TO COME.

Those with limited means should endeavour to arrive in the country as early in spring as possible, say during the month of April, or early in May, so as to have time to hunt up and locate their land. (Guides for this purpose are furnished by the Government to parties free of expense.) By arriving at this time, they have a season of seven months before them, in which to get some of their land under cultivation, build a house, and gather a crop for family use, before winter comes on; to the poor man, who expects his support from the soil, the value of time is an important consideration; as a rule, the autumn is the worst time he could come.

FIRST OPERATIONS.

If the immigrant reaches his land by the middle of May, he can at once break up a few acres, and sow wheat, oats, barley, &c., realizing a fair crop. If he does not commence until the middle of June, he is too late to produce most crops the same season, but he is yet in time for barley, potatoes and turnips. The best time for breaking the prairie sod is in June or July, when the grass roots being filled with juice, a thorough rotting of the turf is secured, and if turned early in June, potatoes may be dropped into the furrow, and covered by the plough with the tough sod, and will grow through it ; the yield will be about half a crop. Indian corn may also be planted on the sod, while turnip seed may be sown, and very slightly covered ; but the ground will be in better condition for the succeeding year where nothing is planted upon the turf. In the following spring the ground should be thoroughly harrowed, and the wheat drilled in or sown broadcast. If sown in May it will be ready for the reaper early in August, and as soon as it is taken off, ploughing may commence for the next year's crop. An early variety of Indian corn should be used. After the furrow is turned, it may be planted by chopping a place with a single stroke of the hatchet, dropping the corn in, and pressing it down with the foot. Squashes, pumpkins, and melons grow on the sod. Beans also may be grown on the turf, and by using early varieties of seed, an abundant supply of these articles of food may be raised for the use of the family. A great advantage to the new settler in having a good yoke of oxen is, that they will work better in the breaking plough, and grow fat on the green grass that they eat at night; whereas, the horses, accustomed to a liberal supply of oats, will not do so well at first on grass alone. A tent may be used to live in at first to gain time in putting in crop.

WHAT IS REQUIRED TO START WITH AND THE COST OF A HOME.

The question is often asked, how much money is indispensably necessary for the settler to get a fair start with? The answer to this depends very much upon who the questioner is, what family he has, with how little they could be content, and many other circumstances which cannot be anticipated. It is therefore best to tell simply *what may be done*, under ordinary adventitious circumstances. In the case of a poor man going on Government land—1st. The entry fee for his homestead of 160 acres will be $10 ; a tent, $12 ; material for his house, if built of sawn lumber, size 16x18 feet, say $125. The work he can do himself, and for winter this can be made warm enough by building a sod wall outside of the boards. Furniture, consisting of a cooking stovee, crockeryware, half a dozen chairs, on table, and two beadsteads (bringing his own bedding), will require about $40. To work his farm, a yoke of oxen, $130 ; a breaking plough, $20 ; waggon, $75 ; total, $392. If he begins in the spring, he can grow corn, potatoes, and garden vegetables, but will have to buy flour for a family of four persons, say $40 ; groceries, $20 ; a cow, $40 ; total, $85. Add for two or three hogs, hoes, shovel, rake, scythe, and other incidentals, say $40, and we have the following :

Entry Fee for homestead.................................	$ 10
Tent	12
Material for house......................................	125
Furniture (exclusive of bedding)........................	40
Farm implements and oxen	225
Living the first 16 months, if no wheat sown..............	100
Incidentals	40
	$552

equal to £110 8s. stg.

or, he may even manage to get along on a lesser sum, by doing with fewer implements at first ; for instance, say :

One Yoke of Oxen	$120.00
One Waggon	80.00
Plough and Harrow	25.00
Chains, Axes, Shovels, etc.	30.00
Stoves, Beds, etc.	60.00
House and Stable, say	150.00

equal to £93 Stg. $465.00

If all his time is not employed about his own claim, he may safely calculate upon having opportunity to work for his neighbours, and earn considerable, or the construction of the Canadian Pacific and other railways will afford him all the employment he desires. The above calculation is of course only intended for the guidance of the poor man.

THE SECOND YEAR OF SETTLEMENT.

He will require cash for seed wheat, and a drag to harrow it in, say $75 ; this year he may confidently expect from his fifty acres of wheat 1,000 bushels. Deducting 200 bushels for bread and seed, and selling the remainder at say 60 cents per bushel, will bring him $480 ; his cash expenses may be limited to groceries, clothing, &c., say $150, and he has $330 to improve his house, and add to his stock and farm implements. If he breaks fifty acres again this year, and secures a crop of say 2,000 bushels (a low average) the third year, the accomplishment of which depends mainly upon his own industry, he will be able to make himself and family comfortable and have a good home. All such as have more money than the sum given above, will not be under the necessity of submitting to so many privations at first, but it may be added, three things are necessary for SUCCESS in any country. They are INDUSTRY, ECONOMY AND CAREFUL BUSINESS MANAGEMENT.

IMPLEMENTS NEEDED, PRICES, &C.

For the information of those with more ample means, and desiring to farm on a larger scale, the following is added as a detailed list of present prices at Winnipeg :—

Waggons complete	$ 70 to	$ 90
Extra Prairie Breaking Plough	20 to	25
Cross Plough, 13 inches	17 to	20
Cultivators, 5 teeth	7 to	9
Harrows, iron with 60 teeth	15 to	20
Sulky Plough	60 to	65
(These Sulky Ploughs are much in use, saving the labour of walking, the horses being driven as in a waggon)		
Sulky Ploughs, 2 gangs	115	
Seeders	75 to	95
Reaping Machine	120 to	140
Farming Mills	35 to	45
Self-Binding Harvester Combined Reaper	300 to	320

(which is supplanting all others, as one man with one of these will accomplish the work of six men with the reaper of six years since).

Nails, 5 cents per lb.
Iron, 7 " "

IN BUILDING MATERIAL.

Common pine lumber, per 1000 ft.............. $25.00 to $30.00
Flooring .... 35.00 to 40.00
Siding (for outside).................................... 35.00 to 40.00
Window Sashes from.................................... 1.50 to 3.00
   "   Frames.. 1.25 to 2.00
Panel doors.. 1.80 to 2.50

COST OF BREAKING AND WORKING LAND.

The following is as near correct an estimate of the cost of operating a prairie farm in Manitoba, or the North-West, and the methods of farming, as we can give :—

Breaking from June 1st to July 20th, cost per acre.........$2.50 to $ 3.00
Backsetting, same breaking in August and September, per acre....... 2.00
Seeding (getting seed in the ground following spring) per acre...... 0.75
Cutting, Binding and Shocking at harvest, per acre..................... 2.50
Cost of raising one acre of wheat, say. 10.75
Twenty bushels (low estimate) wheat at 70 cents 14.00
Profit per acre on first crop, in round numbers....................... 4.75

Hauling to market costs about half a cent per bushel for every mile.

For subsequent years it will be the same as above, less the cost of breaking, $3.00 per acre, and there will be an increase in yield of 10 per cent. a year for three years, where it remains for ten years following.

FENCING.

It has become an established custom among farmers in most of the municipalities, to herd cattle during the summer, confining them in small yards at night. Two or three boys can thus take care of the cattle and sheep of an entire neighborhood. This obviates the necessity of fencing the fields in which grain is growing, and limits the amount of fencing required to what is necessary for enclosing only a few acres about the houses and stabling. This saving becomes considerable, in comparison with which, the cost of herding the stock is insignificant, and in the meantime the appearance of the farm is improved by the absence of unsightly fences. Where suitable fencing timber is scarce, a three string wire fence is at present in general use, the cost being very reasonable.

An excellent plan, much adopted in Minnesota, is planting trees along the highways ; it takes only a few years to grow live fences, which can easily be made to turn cattle into, by placing poles along, and nailing them to the growing trees : Resort to these expedients greatly lessens the force of the objection urged against prairie countries, for there the expense of fencing must always be a serious consideration, especially with those who possess only small capital, if the necessity exists, (as in some localities) for fencing to protect the growing crops against cattle. Legislation has already liberally provided for the encouragement of the growth of timber ; we therefore submit the following :—

INFORMATION ON TREE CULTURE.

As it is a matter of importance that every immigrant in the North-West should endeavor to increase instead of decrease the wood he may have on his farm, as it is a fixed fact in Physical Geography that the more the land in clothed with trees the greater the rainfall. In Palestine and Northern Africa, what were the most fruitful countries in the world 2,000 years ago are now barren wastes. The cause is well known : the trees were cut down, none were planted in their place, the sun evaporated the rain before it had time to permeate the soil, and in course of time the land was given up to perpetual barrenness.

At the same time it may be well to remark that with us the long rich grass which clothes the prairies must act as a great preventive against the sun's power.

The agent which has caused the destruction of forests that once occupied many parts of the prairies is undoubtedly fire, occasioned by the carelessness of travellers and Indians camping, and the same swift and effectual destroyer prevents the new growth from acquiring dimensions, which would enable it to check their annual progress.

This, however, will soon be arrested with advance of settlement and governmental care. In the State of Minnesota, forests have sprung up with wonderful rapidity on the prairies, as the country became settled so as to resist and subdue the encroachment of annual fires.

In view of the importance of the subject, the following practical hints are offered, and will be found of value to the immigrant.

Here is the experience of an extensive farmer in the State of Minnesota; his example can be equally well followed in any part of our prairie lands :

In spring he covered seventy-two acres with cuttings of cotton wood, poplar and white willow, which have flourished finely, and, after two years, were from ten to fourteen feet high. At the same time he *planted several bushels of seed*, including two elder, oak, white and red elm, hard and soft maple and bass wood, and the sprouts from this seed in two years were three to five feet high.

DIRECTIONS FROM EXPERIENCE.   PREPARATION OF THE SOIL.

A proper and thorough cultivation of the soil is an indisputable pre-requisite to success; without this thorough preparation, failure and disappointment are inevitable.

To secure the best results the ground must have been previously broken and the sod thoroughly decomposed, then, with a common stirring plough, the ground to be planted should be given a thorough ploughing to the depth of ten inches, after which it should be thoroughly harrowed until the ground is completely pulverized. It is recommended that the ground for a single row for a fence or for a hedge should be prepared in the above manner, in a strip eight feet wide, in the centre of which the cuttings should be set in, leaving a margin for cultivation four feet wide on each side of the cuttings.

METHOD OF PLANTING.

Stretch a small rope of suitable length over the exact place where it is desirable to plant the cuttings, each end of the rope to be staked firmly to the ground. The ground immediately beneath the rope should be smoothed off with a small iron rake. The planter should then take up as many cuttings as he can conveniently carry under one arm and proceed to stick them in the ground close up to the rope. They should be stuck deep, leaving not more in any case than two buds out of the ground. If stuck in the full length it is just as well. It is advised that they should be stuck in standing say at the angle of from 30 to 45 degrees and invariably butt end first. For a live fence or hedge, they should be struck as nearly as possible one foot apart, 5280 cuttings will plant a mile of such fence. Two good hands can plant this mile in a day if the ground is partly prepared for them.

METHOD OF CULTIVATION.

As soon after planting as the weeds and grass show themselves, hoeing should be commenced; every cutting should be carefully hoed. All of the four feet margin on each side of the row should be hoed thoroughly, as soon afterwards as the cuttings have started, so that the row may be distinctly seen, the grass and weeds killed, leaving all of the four feet on each side of the row perfectly mellow. This process should be repeated two or three times during the season, as not a weed or a bunch of grass should be allowed to go to seed. Great care should be exercised in hoeing not to disturb the cutting of the young tree. After harvest all the weeds and grass found within the four feet margin should be gathered and burned.

Look out for prairie fires, and, if the plantation is in danger, *burn round it.*

It cannot be sufficiently impressed upon the tree planter *that thorough* cultivation the first season will ensure the success of the plantation. The second year the plants will do with half the cultivation, and the third year no further cultivation will be required. By pursuing this treatment the cuttings will be grown in five years to a size and height which will form an impenetrable barrier to horses and cattle, as well as a valuable windbreak. Ten acres planted in this way in rows eight feet apart will in that period (5 years) not only furnish all the fuel and fencing necessary to support a farm, but will also bring a handsome income from the fence poles which may be spared to less fortunate neighbors.

The earlier the cuttings are planted after the frost is out of the ground the better, but the planting may be continued to the 1st of June with success. Cuttings set in spring ploughing time should have the earth pressed on each side of them as fast as the planting progresses.

The cuttings may be procured from the nearest natural groves or belts of woods on the margin of streams or the river sides.

YOUNG TREES AND SEEDS.

Young aspen and poplar, one or two years old, may be gathered in waggon loads on the prairie in the vicinity of groves which fires have not run over. The seeds of the ash-leaved maple, the ash and the elm (very pretty and suitable for protection round the house and stables) may be found in abundance from these trees along the margins of the streams, and should be gathered as soon as ripe. Soft maple and elm ripens in June, and should be planted before the seeds are dried, or they fail to come up; the seed should be planted in drills in small furrows previously made by the hoe, and should be liberally sown, then covered with a small iron rake to a depth of from one to two inches. Seed necessary to be kept throughout the winter should be kept in moist sand, in boxes or barrels, two parts of sand to one of seed, and where they will be kept cool, and at about their natural moisture.

PLAN FOR A SETTLERS' HOUSE.

A very comfortable house, large enough for a family of several persons, may be built at a cost of $236, or about £47 4s. stg. It would be 16 ft. 20 inside, contain a living room 13 x 16, bedroom 7 x 12, pantry 4 x 7, on the ground floor, with stairs leading to the attic. The studding would be twelve feet from the sills to the eaves, the lower storey eight feet, four feet above with a sloping roof will give an attic large enough for good sleeping accommodation. The house would need five windows, one outside and two

2

inside doors. The items of expense would be approximately as follows, not including assistant labour that may be required.

4,000 feet common lumber, at $30	$120.00
4,000 shingles, at $6	24.00
Nails, &c.	20.00
Sheathing paper (to make air tight)	20.00
Doors, windows, &c	24.00
For contingencies, say	28.00
Total	$236.00

The following diagram shows the arrangement of the interior—ground floor.

PLAN—Scale 3-16ths of an inch to the foot.

The eaves should project a foot or more to carry the rain from the sides of the building,—until bricks can be obtained for the chimney, a joint of stove pipe will serve instead, only great care should be taken to protect the surrounding wood from taking fire. The plan is drawn on a scale of 3-16ths of an inch to the foot, so that a settler with the plan before him, may make his own calculations, and be his own joiner. The house should front towards the East or West. The winds prevailing in Manitoba are from the North and South-West. Easterly storms do not often occur. In building the house, oaken posts at each corner, five to six feet in length, and eight or ten inches in diameter, should be sunk into the ground nearly their full length, and the sills spiked firmly to them. This, with proper bracing, will give sufficient firmness to the structure, against the strong winds which often prevail on the prairie. In the autumn, it should be well banked round with manure or earth, with battened walls (strips to cover the seams), and sheathing paper (a kind of thick pasteboard) ; such a house is very warm, and will give good accommodation, till the owner is in circumstances to replace it with one of more ample dimensions.

THE COLONY SYSTEM.

The system of emigrating in small colonies will be found very advantageous to the pioneers, as well as economical ; neighbours in the old land may be neighbours in the new ; friends may settle near each other, form communities and the nucleus of new settlements and towns, establish schools and, in short, avoid many of the traditional hardships which have usually attended pioneer life. The colony system is also calculated to supply the needs of all members of the community, and to furnish employment to every industry. Whenever a colony is established there will soon be near its centre the storekeeper, blacksmith, carpenter, etc., post office, school house and church, and, with the progress of the Canadian Pacific Railway and Steamboat navigation, a market. Until then an ample market, commanding high prices, is created in the interior by the influx of following settlers and the rapidly increasing trade.

The attention of the capitalist intending to emigrate is drawn to the importance and mutual advantage of this system, in which capital, directed by sagacity and enterprise, possesses such unquestionable advantages, united with industry and a plucky purpose, and in no place under the sun could it reap better rewards than under the bright skies and healthful atmosphere of this fair land.

IMPORTANT MISCELLANEOUS INFORMATION.

WHAT CAPITAL CAN DO.

Of course capital, directed by sagacity and enterprise, possesses great advantages here as elsewhere ; indeed, the numerous avenues being continually opened up by the rapid development of a bountiful new country like this, multiply the opportunities for its profitable employment. There is scarcely a vocation of any kind wherein the same capital and good management which insures success in older communities will not yield far greater returns here. The legal rate of interest when not stipulated, is six per cent ; but any rate agreed to is lawful varying from ten to twenty per cent. At the latter rate money may be safely loaned, amply secured by mortgage. Judicious investments in real estate, owing to the rapid settlement and development of the country are sure to realize large profits. Purchasers, both of city lots and farming lands, can be made in the Province of Manitoba at all times, which will command an advance of 25 to 50 per cent. within a year, and not unfrequently such advance is over 100 per cent annually. The time was a few years ago, when this could be done without discrimination by the venturer, the sole condition of acquiring fancied wealth being to take hold. Now, good judgment is required to cause real estate or any active business to yield much better returns than money commands at interest.

WHAT PLUCK AND MUSCLE MAY DO.

Great as are the unquestionable advantages which a union of money and industry possess, there is no country under the sun where unaided muscle, with a plucky purpose, reaps greater rewards than under the bright skies and helpful atmosphere of this fair land.

Feeling himself every inch a man, as he gazes upon the unclaimed acres which shall reward his toil, the settler breathes a freer air, his bosom swells with a prouder purpose, and his strong arms achieve unwonted results. Any man whose capital consists on his arrival of little but brawny arms and a brave heart, may do as others have done before him, select a homestead in some of the many beautiful and fertile regions westward, and into which railroads will rapidly penetrate; after which, being allowed six months before settling upon the land, he may work upon the railroad and earn enough of money to make a start in a small way; and by the time he produces a surplus, the railway will be within a reasonable distance to take it to market; he finds himself the proud possessor of a valuable farm, which has cost him little but the sweat of his brow.

PUBLIC LANDS.

Under the provisions of the Dominion Public Lands' Act (*for which, see official notice at end*), a vast area of land abounding in all the elements of health, beauty, and fertility, of much greater extent than many of the principalities of Europe, is open for the landless of all nations of the earth, to enter upon and possess, who may be the head of a family, male or female, or who has attained the age of eighteen years, may become the owner of a farm of 160 acres without paying for it, by simply cultivating and residing upon the land for three years, and the land thus acquired without cost (with the exception of the office fee for entry, of $10), is exempt by law from liabilities for all debts previously contracted, thereby showing that we have no limitation as to the value of the farm or residence thus secured to the family; whatever its value *may become*, it remains the shelter, the castle, the home of the family, to cluster round in the hour of gloom and disaster, as securely as they were wont to do in the sunshine of prosperity. Such an exemption law will be found a blessing to thousands of worthy men, women and children.

Here every man may enjoy the reward of his labor, and become an independent land proprieto. However poor, he may possess equal rights, and equal political opportunities, with the rich and prosperous.

All information as to the nature of particular localities, where the immigrant may desire to settle, will be afforded him for his guidance by the officers of the Dominion Lands Branch of the Department of Interior at Winnipeg, or any of the district officers.

SYSTEM OF SURVEYS.

Each township consists of thirty-six sections of one square mile each, and road allowances, of one chain in width between all townships and sections.

Sections are numbered 1 to 36, and a raised mound of turf with picket marked, being at each corner of section.

PRIVATE LANDS.

Farms of various degrees of improvement, near a town, are frequently offered for sale at from $5 to $15 per acre, such price being often less than the cost of the buildings and fences. These cases occur not from the undesirable character of the property, so much as from the restlessness and ove of change, characteristic of the people of the country. The Hudson's

Bay Company are the owners, under the Dominion Lands Act, of two sections in every surveyed township in the great fertile belt. Each section consists of 640 acres, and is sold either in block or in quarter sections of 160 acres each ; the prices of these lands are regulated according to location and quality, ranging from $4 per acre and upwards, with easy terms of payment. During the past year 35,000 acres were sold at an average price of $6 per acre.

RAILROAD LANDS.

As this pamphlet may be read by many in Great Britain, who are unacquainted with the meaning of the term "railroad lands," we deem it important to offer a few words by way of explanation. All the lands are originally the property of the Crown, and are granted to aid in the construction of railways, as experience has shown that a locomotive running through a new country tends as much to civilize it as to settle it up ; the wisdom of this disposal of lands by the Government of Canada can only be commended. Such lands are situate along the lines of road to which they were granted, and consist of the odd numbered sections (the even numbered sections being for free homestead entry as Government lands), on both sides of the line for a certain number of miles. The title to such lands are good, coming directly from the Crown to the Railway Company.

The Canadian Pacific Railway Company offer lands in the Fertile Belt of Manitoba and the North-West Territory, for sale, on certain conditions as to cultivation, at the price of $2.50 (10s. stg.) per acre, one-sixth payable in cash, and the balance in five annual instalments, with interest at six per cent., a rebate of fifty per cent., for actual cultivation being made as hereinafter described.

The ordinary conditions of sale are :—

1. That all improvements placed upon land purchased shall remain thereon until final payment for the land has been made.

2. That all taxes and assessments lawfully imposed upon the land or improvements shall be paid by the purchaser.

3. The Company reserve from selection at the above price all mineral, coal, or wood-lands, stone, slate and marble quarries, lands with water-power thereon, and tracts for town sites and railway purposes ; and, as regards lands having some standing wood, but not hereby excluded from selection, the purchaser will only be permitted to cut a sufficient quantity for fuel, fencing, and for the erection of buildings on his land until he shall have received the final conveyance thereof.

Manitoba has already unbroken connection by Railway to all parts of the Continent of America ; and the Canadian Pacific Railway is already pushed nearly three hundred miles west of Winnipeg, and will reach the Rocky Mountains in less than two years. The Canadian Pacific Railway connection between Thunder Bay and Winnipeg will open for traffic this year, that arduous work being nearly completed. This will give independent Canadian communication between the Eastern Provinces and the North-West during the season of navigation. Other lines of railway, within the North-West are being pushed rapidly forward.

Colonization Railways are being projected in every direction ; and it is proposed to open up another outlet to Europe *via* Hudson's Bay.

COAL LANDS.

The route of the Canadian Pacific Railway is indicated as the natural pathway of Commerce, by the vast and inexhaustible coal beds through which it runs for over two hundred miles. From Geological reports, and the Engineer's surveys, the district through which it passes possesses one of the largest coal fields in the world.

Between the 59th parallel and the North Sea, it has been calculated that there cannot be much less than 500,000 square miles that are underlaid by true coal. The average breadth of this belt is about 280 miles. In addition to the coal, this country contains rich deposits of iron ore.

On the North Saskatchewan River, coal prevails with little interruption in beds two and two-and-a-half feet thick on the bank of the river, from a little below Edmonton, upwards for two hundred miles.

On the Pembina River, seventy miles to the west, there is a seam ten feet thick, of a very superior quality. On the Battle River it is also noted, and in the Red Deer Branch of the South Saskatchewan, 170 miles from its mouth, are extensive deposits of coal, and at 100 miles further up it is there in beds so close, that, of 20 feet of strata exposed, 12 feet are coal.

Coal has lately been discovered on the Souris River, at a point near the international boundary line, and the South-Western Railway is now under construction to connect that point with the City of Winnipeg, a distance of nearly 200 miles, through a magnificent and exceedingly fertile country.

The Minister of the Interior has the power to protect persons desiring to carry on coal mining in the possession of the lands on which such mining may be carried on, provided the proper application is made, with a deposit of one dollar per acre, under the terms of the Dominion Lands Act.

HAY AND GRAZING LANDS.

The wild grasses of Manitoba and the North-West, extending to the foot of the Rocky Mountains, are famous for the nourishment they contain. They not only afford rich and ample pasturage upon which horses, cattle and sheep may thrive well, but also make an excellent quality of hay ; many farmers prefer them to timothy for the latter purpose. Three varieties, the buffalo and herd grass and the blue joint, after the ground has been mowed over a few times, become fine and succulent, and cure very nicely, and even the coarsest variety of slough glass is similarly affected, though its improvement is not so marked. Cattle subsist during the winter on hay of this latter description, and keep in good order. For the encouragement of persons desirous of going into stock-raising on a large scale, the Government is empowered und. · the Lands Act to grant leases of unoccupied Dominion Lands for grazing purposes to any person, for such term of years, and at such rent in each case as may be deemed expedient, conditionally, that the Minister of the Interior may, on giving two years' notice, cancel the lease at any time during the term.

MINERAL RESOURCES.

Our mineral deposits—next in importance to coal, already referred to —may, so far as yet known, be embraced in the following :

Iron—Is found throughout the coal region, at accessible distances from the line of railway, and gives promise of the establishment of future centres of industry along the line of the Canadian Pacific Railway.

Gold—Is found on the numerous sand-bars of the North Saskatchewan River, paying from $5 to $10 per day, with limited appliances for mining and washing. As the country settles up, and supplies become cheaper and more easily obtained, no doubt enterprising proprietors will yet make valuable discoveries in the numerous streams running from the eastern slope of the Rocky Mountains.

Rich gold and silver-bearing quartz veins have recently been discovered on some of the thousands of the islands which dot the beautiful Lake of the Woods ; the discoverers have as yet, from want of capital. been unable to properly develop these mines ; but when the attention of capitalists is attracted, no doubt future enterprise will cause operations to be conducted on a large scale, supporting a numerous mining population. A portion of the Pacific Railway is now completed and running to Rat Portage, a thriving little town at the head of the Lake, east from Winnipeg 136 miles.

Limestone—A fine quality is found in many portions of the country, and affords ample material for the manufacture of lime.

Clay—A kind of blue clay, underlying the soil, makes brick of a good quality. White marl occurs in large beds ; it is used for pottery-making, and also makes a hard, durable brick, similar to the famous Milwaukee brick.

Salt Springs—Are numerous—some of them very pure, yielding upwards of a bushel of salt to thirty or forty gallons of brine, the writer having himself made salt from the brine of that strength as obtained on the surface without boring, and of as good a quality, as American or English production. With the development of the country, this source of wealth must yet be an important one.

DESCRIPTIVE AND GENERAL.

THE SOIL AND ITS AGRICULTURAL CAPACITY.

The soil is generally an alluvial black argillaceous mould, rich in organic deposit, and resting for a depth of eighteen inches to four feet, on a tenacious clay. Scientific analysis develops the presence in due proportion of elements of extraordinary fertility, comparing favorably with the most celebrated soils of the world. This theoretic excellence is amply confirmed by the practical results of agriculture, as is shewn hereafter.

The following important analysis of a sample of the prairie soil of this country, was made at the instigation of some gentlemen of capital, practical farmers in Scotland, who visited the country, and became so favorably impressed as to invest largely in lands.

The analysis is by Dr. Macadam, the well-known lecturer on Chemistry in the University of Edinburgh, and proves beyond doubt that to the

24

farmer who desires to select for his future home a country which has the most productive soil, and promises the richest harvest, nowhere in the world are greater attractions offered:

ANALYTICAL LABORATORY, SURGEON'S HALL,

EDINBURGH, 14th December, 1876.

ANALYSIS OF SAMPLE OF MANITOBA SOIL.

Moisture		21.364
Organic matter containing nitrogen equal to ammonia, 23°		11.223
Saline matter :		
Phosphates	0.472	
Carbonate of lime	1.763	
Carbonate of magnesia	0.937	
Alkaline salts	1.273	
Oxide of iron	3.115	
		7.560
Silicious matter :		
Sand and silica	51.721	
Alumina	8.132	
		59.853
		100.000

The above soil is very rich in organic matter, and contains the full amount of the saline fertilizing matters found in all soils of a good bearing quality.

(Signed),   STEPHENSON MACADAM, M. D.

Lecturer on Chemistry, &c.

An important feature in the soil of our prairies is, that its earthy materials are minutely pulverised, and is almost everywhere light, mellow, and spongy.

With these uniform characteristics, the soils are of different grades of fertility, according to local situation. The limestone sub-strata of this region, with its rich, deep, calcareous loam and retentive clay sub-soil, is always associated with a rich wheat development, while its hot and humid summers fulfil all the climatological conditions of a first-rate wheat country. Some fields on the Red River have been known to produce twenty successive crops of wheat without fallow or manure, and the yield has frequently reached as high as forty bushels per acre.

Blodgett (an American authority) states "that the basin of the Winnipeg is the seat of the greatest average wheat product on this continent, and probably *in the world.*"

As will be observed by the analysis of Dr. Macadam, a general ingredient of the soil is sand, of which silica is the base, as of all good soils. It plays an important part in the economy of growth, and is an essential constituent in the organism of all cereals. We are told that about 67 per cent. of the ash of the stems of wheat, corn, rye, barley, oats, &c., is pure silica, or flint. It is this which gives the glazed coating to the plants and gives strength to the stain. Now this silica is an acid and is insoluble, but readily combines with lime, soda, magnesia, potash, and the other ingredients of our soil, and in this condition is readily available to the use of the plant.

and forms an essential element in the growth of the cereals ; from this and other causes is attributable the superiority of our wheat over all other grown East or South.

WHEAT GROWING.

The average yield of wheat in Manitoba, deduced from the aggregate of local estimates, is twenty-five bushels to the acre, the range of ordinary yields being from fifteen to thirty-five. Experience has taught us to allow largely for the disposition to base general inferences on the most striking and notorious instances, and for the general habit of confounding a usual result with an average one.

A comparison of the yield of wheat for past years in Manitoba with the best diitricts of the United States, will show its superiority over them, viz :—

Red River Spring Wheat, average production, 25 bushels per acre.
Minnesota	do	do	20	do	do
Wisconsin	do	do	14	do	do
Pennsylvania	do	do	15	do	do
Massachusetts	do	do	16	do	do

The weight as compared with the following States, is :

Manitoba Spring Wheat		...............63 to 66 lbs. to the bushel.	
Minnesota	do	...............60 to 65 lbs.	do
Illinois	do	.... 52 to 58 lbs.	do
Ohio	do	...............57 to 60 lbs.	do
Pennsylvania	do	....57 to 60 lbs.	do

The soundness and fulness of the grain is unmistakeably indicated by the fact, that it *will command a higher price* than any Western State grain, when it goes to market unmixed and well cleaned.

The fact established by climatologists that " the cultivated plants, yield the greatest products near the Northermmost limit, at which they will grow " is fully illustrated in our productions.

An extensive Miller in Minnesota. was astonished on visiting Manitoba,. at the yield of wheat in his hand. " We have had an excellent harvest in Minnesota, but I never saw more than two well formed grains in each group, or cluster, forming a row, *but here, the rate is three grains in each cluster. That's the difference between twenty and thirty bushels per acre.*"

Winter wheat has not been tried, except in one or two instance, the result being unfavorable to its reputation as a reliable crop ; and an opinion is generally prevelant, that it cannot be grown successfully ; but this opinion is not warranted by facts. The success of winter wheat depends peculiarly upon having a moderate and sure covering of light snow, not condensed by thaws, and packed close by warm winds. Such a snowy covering requires—firstly, a moderate fall of snow ; and secondly, a low, uniform range of temperature, free from winter rains and prolonged thaws, sufficient to dissipate the snowy covering.

These are, in fact, the decided characteristics of our winters. The precipitation of snow at Manitoba is about 25 inches for the whole winter.

It is remarkable also that light falls coincide with quite low temperatures. The short noon-day heats, which often carry the thermometer for an hour or two above freezing point in winter, are not sufficient to create a thaw, and even a whole day, but slightly above, freezing, will not seriously affect the snow.

Wheat-growing has been termed the "back-bone of agriculture." When the vital importance of maintaining and increasing the production of a grain so essential to civilized man is considered, it cannot be assigned a less place in agricultural economy. Wheat is pre-eminently the food of civilized nations ; and perhaps there can be no surer measure of their civilization than the culture and consumption of that cereal. History affirms its agency in shaping the power and character of nations. They have grown sturdy and progressive in their ratio of wheat consumption by all classes. Scientific analysis confirms the indications of history. Anatomy and Chemistry show that food to be best, which gives toughness to muscular fibre, and tone to the brain.

England, who has long since been the conceded mistress of the seas, and whose dependencies will nigh encircle the globe, has so stimulated and enlarged her capacity for wheat-growing, that her annual average is twenty-eight bushels per acre ; but her consumption so far outruns her production, that she lays the world under contribution for her supplies of bread. The grave significance of the question involved is not susceptible of conceal-ment, when the fact is considered that while the consumption of wheat, as the choice food of the human race, is rapidly extending, the capacity of wheat-growing regions for its production is rapidly diminishing. We are told that in New England, U.S., the entire wheat product of a year is barely sufficient to feed her own people for three weeks, and the State of New York for six months. In the ten years ending in 1860, the wheat crop of only four States decreased 6,500,000 bushels. In the light of these facts it is not difficult to foresee that the North-West of the Dominion of Canada must yet assume a proud pre-eminency in wheat-growing.

The following facts are demonstrated :

First.—That there exists a constantly and inevitably increasing foreign demand for breadstuffs, with a constantly increasing demand for domestic consumption.

Second.—That therefore the value of wheat, as a commercial staple, is advancing in a compound ratio.

Third.—That, within this zone, the climate and other causes tend to concentrate the growth of wheat in the best districts.

Fourth.—The prairie lands of Canada are the best of these wheat districts, having the largest average yield, the most certain crops, and the best and healthiest grains.

STOCK RAISING.

The experience of many years shows that no physical impediment arising from climate or soil, exists to prevent the prairies of our North-

West becoming one of the best grazing countries in the world, and with the introduction of immigration, in a few years, the beautiful prairies of the North-West will be enlivened by numerous flocks and herds, and the cattle trade, already springing into importance, will rapidly increase. It is understood that a prominent member of the Senate of Canada is at present making arrangements to enter upon the raising of thorough-bred stock, horned cattle, horses, sheep and pigs, and with that view, is now in treaty with the Government of the Dominion for the purchase and lease respectively of very considerable tracts of grazing land near the foot of the Rocky Mountains, for a stock farm. For raising cattle and horses, this country is equal to the State of Illinois, and for sheep-raising it is far superior. The quality of the beef and mutton raised upon our northern grasses, has been pronounced of superior excellence. Among the peculiar advantages of Manitoba for stock-raising and wool-growing, the most prominent are—1st. The richness and luxuriance of the native grasses. The grass is mainly cut on the swamps and meadows, which chequer the prairies, or fringe the streams and lakes. 2nd. The great extent of unoccupied land, affording for many years to come, a wide range of free pasturage. 3rd. The remarkable dryness and healthfulness of the winter. The cold dry air sharpens the appetite, and promotes a rapid secretion of fat, and vigorous muscular development. All point to stock-raising as one of the most important and promising of the diversified channels into which the industry of the immigrant and capitalist is to be ected. Notwithstanding the expensiveness and difficulty of stocking farms in a new country like this, where animals must be procured at a distance of hundreds of miles, the progress already made in this direction affords a gratifying proof of the rapid growth of this important interest.

SHEEP AND WOOL GROWING.

There is not room in this guide to give the subject of wool growing the attention which its importance deserves. The experience of forty years, and of some who have been engaged in the business in Australia, establishes beyond a reasonable doubt the following conclusions :

1.—That from the nature of our climate and the general undulating character of the prairies, the richness of the grasses, and the purity of the waters, this country is adapted in an eminent degree to the healthful and profitable breeding of sheep.

2.—That sheep are entire'y free from the diseases which cut them off, so largely in more southern climates.

3.—That the characteristic dryness of our winters, not only protects them from the casualities to which they are exposed in moister winter climates, but stimulates them to a more healthy and vigorous growth.

4.—That the naturalization of sheep imported from Illinois, Ohio, and other middle states of America, *improves the quality of their wool.*

5.—That it is by *far the most profitable branch of industry in which the settler with capital can engage,* especially in connection with stock-raising.

Prolific as is the soil, it is far from the Eastern markets, and the bulky and weighty products of the field largely consume themselves in the cost of transit. Wheat which is bought here for 60 cents, sells for 90 cents or $1.00 in Montreal or New York, costing the farmer 30 to 40 cents for transportation. A few years, it is true, will complete a great system of internal improvement by means of the Canadian Pacific Railway. But even then, it will be far more profitable to grow wool ; the best information on this subject shows that it costs about 15 cents to produce a pound of wool, which sells here for 30 cents, yielding a net profit of 15 cents per pound, and mutton at present commands from 12½ to 15 cents per pound! The cost of producing a bushel of wheat varies with the yield, the average cost being about $6.50 per acre, or about 32 cents per bushel for an average yield of 20 bushels to the acre. The average product of wool is not subject to fluctuation, and the price also is far steadier than that of breadstuffs. Well-fed ews produce fleeces from 3 to 3½ pounds. Wethers produce fleeces from 6 to 8 pounds, the wool being of good quality. All breeds stand the winter cold well, but the Cotswold the best. An instance came to the knowledge of the writer, where a flock of about twenty strayed away in the beginning of winter and were found in the spring fat, and none missing, but an addition to the flock in lambs. An experienced settler writes as follows : "I believe this to be equal to any country for sheep growing. I prefer the Cotswold breed to any other for this country, as they are good shearers, prolific breeders, and good for mutton. My sheep have been troubled with no disease, but the dogs have killed and wounded some. I believe that in this branch of husbandry this country has few equals, and no superiors in any country of the globe."

To simply raise a crop of wheat from the new prairie, is but one remove from barbarism ; but when we see upon a farm a flock of pure blood sheep, and a herd of well bred cattle, we are sure that behind them all is superior intelligence, and we feel confident the farm is not running out.

DAIRY FARMING

Must also become in a few years an important source of wealth. It is now conducted on a very large scale in the other Provinces, in connection with cheese and butter factories for European consumption. In the Province of Ontario alone no less than 200 cheese factories being in operation, that Province deriving an income of nearly two millions of dollars a year from this single article of produce, and the quality esteemed almost as highly as the best English cheese.

With the progress of improved communications, what a vast field is presented for the development of that branch of agricultural enterprise in this great grazing country.

THE BEET ROOT.

Beet root sugar manufacturing will certainly, at no distant day, be a question of much interest in this part of Canada, and occupy the attention of the capitalist, for without doubt the rich deep mould of our soil is immensely superior to anything upon the continent for the production of the sugar beet.

It is the opinion of the *Monetary Times* that the production of beet root sugar, if prosecuted on a sufficiently large scale, could be made very profitable. A calculation is given, setting forth the estimated results of the manufacture of a thousand tons of sugar beets in the States of New York and Pensylvania, as made by an American gentleman who has given long consideration to the subject. It is as follows :

EXPENSES.

1000 tons of beets at $4 per ton	$4,000
Estimated cost of manufacture at $5 per ton	5,000
Total	**$9,000**

RESULT.

200 tons pulp at $2 per ton	$ 400
30 " syrup at $20 per ton	600
60 " of sugar at $250 per ton	15,000
Total results	**$16,000**
From which deduct expenses	9,000
Leaves a profit of	**$7,000**

The sugar beet will grow on our prairie soil to great perfection. Those sent from here to Philadelphia were the suprise and admiration of thousands from all parts of the world.

This fact being established, it next becomes important to have a proper test made of the percentage of saccharine matter the beets grown in our soil will yield, and its suitability for manufacture. It is advisable : beets intended for sugar manufacture, should be grown on old ploughed land, rather than the newly ploughed prairie.

This manufacture, which has elsewhere been found so profitable, will probably be found the same in the North-West of Canada.

SALUBRITY OF CLIMATE AND ADAPTION TO AGRICULTURE.

Of paramount importance to the emigrant is the healthfulness of the locality which is to be the scene of his future labors, and the home for himself and family. What to him are fair fields, flowering meadows, buried in the luxuriant growth of fertile soils and tropical suns, if they generate fever-producing miasma and vapour ? What are soft and perfumed breezes, if they waft the seeds of pestilence and death ? What are bountiful harvests of golden grain, rich and mellow fruits, and all the wealth the earth can yield, if disease must annually visit his dwelling, and death take away, one by one, the loved and the young? It is well known that some of the fairest portions of the Western States are so fruitful of the causes of disease as almost to preclude settlement. And thousands have left their comparatively healthy Canadian and European homes to find untimely graves in the prairie soil of Indiana, Illinois, Iowa and Missouri. And even in the sections of these States deemed most healthy, the climate has an enervating effect upon those accustomed to the bracing air of Northern Europe and our Eastern Provinces.

The dryness of the air, the character of the soil, which retains no stagnant pools to send forth poisonous exhalations, and the almost total absence of a fog or mist, the brilliancy of its sunlight, the pleasing succession of its seasons, all conspire to make this a climate of unrivalled salubrity and the home of a joyous, healthy, prosperous people, strong in physical, intellectual and moral capabilities. Therefore, the assertion that the climate of our North-West is one of the healthiest in the world may be broadly and confidently made, sustained by the experience of its inhabitants. Some of the hardiest and strongest men the writer has ever seen are Europeans and Canadians, who came to this country at an early date, and finally became settlers. Agriculture, therefore, cannot suffer from unhealthiness of climate.

Its distinguishing features in relation to husbandry : The melon, growing in open air, and arriving at perfect maturity in August and September. may be briefly explained by reference to the amount of sunlight received during our growing seasons, viz : Whilst at New Orleans in July they have fourteen hours of sunlight, we have sixteen, with much longer twilight than they, consequently our vegetation grows more rapidly than theirs, and matures much sooner. This is a beautiful law in compensation, as what we lack in heat is made up in sunlight during our summers. Changes in our temperature, it must be admitted, are sometimes sudden and violent. We are about half way to the North Pole, and subject to either extremes. This, instead of being a disadvantage, is rather in our favour ; it gives variety, a thing desirable at times. Then, again, these changes are, for the reasons already given, seldom pernicious. Plants and animals are armed with the proper implements for resistance. I would not infer that we are subject to hurricanes, or other violent commotions of the atmosphere, any more or as much as other places. But we have a touch at times of both extremes, a vibratory movement of the climates of the torrid and frigid zones.

The seasons follow each other in pleasing succession. As the sun approaches its northern altitude, winter relaxes its grasp, streams and lakes are unbound, prairie flowers spring up, as if by the touch of some magic wand, and gradually spring is merged into the bright, beautiful June, with its long warm days, and short, but cool and refreshing nights. The harvest months follow in rapid succession, till the golden Indian summer of early November foretells the approach of cold and snow ; and again winter, with its short days of clear, bright sky and bracing air, and its long nights of cloudless beauty, complete the circle.

The average fall of snow is about six inches per month. The snow falls in small quantities, at different times, and is rarely blown into drifts so as to impede travelling. With the new year commences the extreme cold of our winter, when, for a few days, the mercury ranges from 15 to 35 degress below zero, falling sometimes even below that. Yet the severity of these days is much softened by the brilliancy of the sun and the stillness of the air. Thus, while in lower latitudes they are being drenched by the cold rain storms, or buried beneath huge drifts of wintry snow, we enjoy a dry atmosphere, with bright cloudless days and serene starlight nights; and when the moon turns her full orbed face towards the earth, the night scene is one of peerless grandeur.

FROSTS.

Experience has shewn that the liability to disastrous frosts in the season of growth, and which so intimately concerns the interests of husbandry, is not any worse in this country than elsewhere, when the thermometer has occasionally fallen to 30° in the latter end of August; vegetation did not suffer; in fact the injury was scarcely noticeable, which may be accounted for from the following reasons:

1. The dryness of the atmosphere (which is a peculiarity of this region), allows a much lower range of temperature without injury to vegetation, than in moister climates; and in addition to the heat, gives greater vigour to the plants, they grow rapidly but with firm texture, and are consequently able to resist much cold. On account of their excessive vitality, the same as a person who has dined heartily on rich food, is better able to bear the cold of winter.

2. The sudden change of temperature, which is often the case in this region, one extreme following another in rapid succession, is less deleterious to vigorous plants than a gradual lowering of temperature. The earth and plants still retain the heat previously absorbed, and are thus enabled to bear an atmosphere at 20° much better than at 35°, after their latent heat has been given off. The soil of the prairie is in general dry, and is rapidly warmed by the rays of the sun in spring.

3. The dryness of the air is accounted for from the fact that the moisture conveyed in the air has a tendency to soften the delicate covering of the plants, and thus render them more sensitive to cold.

4. The heat retaining character of the soil. For these and several other reasons that might be mentioned, the climate of Manitoba is less subject to killing frosts than might at first be supposed, on account of its high latitude.

SEASONS.

The natural division of the season is as follows:
Spring—April and May.
Summer—June, July, August and part of September.
Autumn—Part of September and October.
Winter—November and December, January, February and March.

Frequently the weather is warm, the atmosphere hazy and calm till late in November, and the early and rapid advancement of temperature in May is strikingly represented.

FRUITS.

The culture of fruit, especially the apple, has been almost entirely neglected heretofore in this region; probably on account of there generally being such an abundance or wild fruits, or the difficulty of procuring cuttings. For this and other reasons an erroneous impression has prevailed that we could not raise fruit or apple orchards—an extraordinary inference, when we consider that many forms of wild fruit are indigenous to the country, abounding in the woodlands, and unsurpassed in flavour, size and productiveness—the principal of which are strawberries, whortleberries, saskatoon, and marsh and high bush cranberries; therefore, immigrants are not likely to suffer for want of fruit.

In Minnesota the wild plum improves so much by being transplanted and cultivated as to equal any of the garden varieties. The high-bush cranberry also improves by transplanting, and makes a beautiful ornament to the grounds about the prairie farmer's house.

The celebrated and delicious apple peculiar to the neighborhood of Montreal, known as the "*Fameuse*," will no doubt be successfully raised here; although we are nearly five degrees further north than Montreal, yet we are twenty-six degrees further west. Some young trees are doing well; as also a variety from nurseries in Minnesota. The "*Fameuse*" is a rich and beautiful apple, peculiar to the climate and soil of the Island of Montreal, a rich loam with a heavy clay subsoil, which retains the rooting, and prevents the growth of the tree pushing ahead too rapidly for the severe frosts of that latitude. It should be borne in mind that it is not the severity of the winter that kills the young apple tree, but the *alternate thawing and freezing* of the south side of the tree in the spring, which can be avoided by mulching and protecting the stem of the tree when young, by a wrapping of straw. With these precautions, and procuring plants from a suitable climate, or planting the seeds, and thus acclimatising, there is no reason why every farm may not have its orchard in this as in other parts of the Dominion.

THE SALAD PLANTS.

Cabbage, lettuce, celery, spinach, &c., are not only more tender with us than in warm climate, where the relaxing sun lays open their very buds, and renders their limbs thin and tough, but are more nutritious, because their growth is slow, and their juices well digested. The cabbage attains enormous size, as also the cauliflower, pumpkins and cucumbers; the latter come in rather late, but instead of throwing too much of their growth into the vine, as they do south, fully mature, and grow very fine and large.

OATS, BARLEY, RYE, POTATOES, ETC.

The whole group of subordinate cereals follow wheat, and are less restricted in their range, growing five degrees beyond wheat, in the Mackenzie River Valley to the Arctic Circle. Barley is a favourite alternative of wheat in Manitoba, and yields enormous returns, with a weight per bushel of from 50 to 55 pounds. Oats also thrive well. Potatoes.—The mealy quality, the snowy whiteness, the farinaceous properties, and the exquisite flavour which distinguish the best article, reach perfection only in high latitudes.

The potatoes grown in Manitoba are well-known to be unsurpassed in all the qualities named, while their prolific yield is not less remarkable. Turnips, parsnips, carrots, beets, and nearly all bulbous plants, do equally as well as potatoes.

FLAX AND HEMP.

The cultivation of these important crops was carried on to a considerable extent by old settlers many years ago, the product being of excellent quality, but the universal complaint at that time was the want of a market, or of machinery to work up the raw material, and this led them to discontinue this important branch of husbandry. Its cultivation is again renewed extensively by the Russian Mennonite settlers, of whom there are now between 8,000 and 10,000 in this country, who within only three or four years, are, by their untiring industry, rapidly gaining the road to wealth.

It is well known that flax and hemp come only to perfection in a cool country; their bark in southern climates is harsh and brittle, because the plant is forced into maturity so rapidly that the lint does not acquire either consistency or tenacity. No doubt the North-West of Canada will prove equal for flax and hemp growth to Northern Europe.

BEES

thrive well in the North-West, as they require a clear dry atmosphere, and a rich harvest of flowers; if the air is damp, or the weather cloudy, they will not work so well. Another reason why they work less in a warm climate is, that the honey gathered remains too fluid for sealing a longer time, and, if gathered faster than it thickens, it sours and spoils. Our clear, bright skies, dry air and rich flora, are well adapted to the bee culture, and, since the process of burying bees during the winter has been introduced successfully in Minnesota, and generally adopted in the North-Western States, the length and coldness of our winter ceases to be an obstacle. In fact, experience in Minnesota proves that bees succeed better there, consume less honey during the winter, and the colony comes out much stronger than in warmer climates.

GAME.

The prairies and forests abound in great variety of wild animals, among which are deer, bears, wolves, foxes, wild-cats, raccoons and rabbits, otter, mink, beaver and muskrat are the principal aquatic animals that frequent the water courses. Buffalo in the Western prairies. Pigeons, grouse, partridges and prairie chickens are among the feathered game. In the fall and spring ducks and geese are found in immense numbers.

FISH.

The larger lakes abound in white fish, a delicious article of food, weighing from four to five pounds. The fisheries of the lakes, when properly developed, will form an important source of revenue. The rivers and streams abound in pickerel, pike, catfish, sturgeon, gold-eyes, &c., and trout in the mountain streams.

BEAUTY AND FERTILITY OF THE NORTH-WEST.

Throughout our prairie lands is found not the illimitable level, treeless prairies which distinguish Illinois, but a charming alternation of woods and prairie, upland and meadow, characterize the topography of the country. The general surface is undulating, well watered, and ample building timber on the main streams. The prairie is frequently interspersed with groves of poplar and oak openings, in many parts numerous lakes, presenting a pleasing and enlivening appearance.

It would be absurd to expect any country of this vast extent to be all equally fit to receive the plough at once. If only one-third is here pointed out as awaiting the industrious hand of man to ensure him independence, the other two-thirds are parts requiring draining or partial clearing. It would also be absurd to suppose it all equally fertile, as there is a considerable difference between the deep beds of black vegetable mould which generally prevail, and of course there are occasional bad spots and poor sandy ground, which must be found in all countries; but prominent among the questions proposed by the emigrant or capitalist seeking a new home in a new country are those concerning the climate, its temperature, adaptation to the culture of the grand staples of food, and its healthfulness. Therefore, in proof of our assertion that the North-West of Canada offers the finest and most inviting field for emigration, the following is submitted as

OFFICIAL AND SCIENTIFIC TESTIMONY.

In 1858, Captain Palliser was requested by the Under Secretary of State for the Colonies to state his opinion on the country he was engaged in exploring, and he describes the region drained by the Saskatchewan in the following words :—

"The extent of surface drained by the Saskatchewan and other tributaries to Lake Winnipeg, which we had an opportunity of examining, amounts in round numbers to one hundred and fifty thousand square miles. This region is bounded to the North by what is known as the strong woods. or the Southern limit of the great circum-arctic zone of forest which occupies the 'atitudes in the Northern Hemisphere. This line, which is indicated on the map, sweeps to the North-West from the shore of Lake Winnipeg, and reaches its most Northerly limit, about 54° 30' N. and l. gitude 119° W., from where it again passes to the South-West, meeting the Rocky M. untains in latitude 51° N. and 115° W. Between this line of the strong woods and the Northern limit of the true prairie country there is a belt of land varying in width, which at one period must have been covered by an extension of the Northern forests, but which has been gradually cleared by successive fires.

"It is now a partially wooded country, abounding in lakes and rich natural pasturage, in some parts rivalling the finest park scenery of our own country. Throughout this region of country the climate seems to possess the same character, although it passes through very different latitudes, its form being doubtless determined by the curves of the isothermal line. Its superficial extent embraces about sixty-five thousand square miles, (whether geographical or statute he does not state; if the former, it would be about eighty-five thousand statute) of which *more than* one-third may be considered as at once available for the purposes of the agriculturist. Its elevation increases from seven hundred to four thousand feet as we approach the Rocky Mountains at Edmonton, which has an altitude of 3,000 feet. Wheat is cultivated with success. The least valuable portion of the Prairie Country has an extent of about eighty thousand square miles, and is that lying along the Southern branch of the Saskatchewan, Southward from thence to the boundary line, while its Northern limit is known in the Indian languages as the "edge of the woods," the original line of the woods being invaded by fire.

"*It is a physical reality of the highest importance to the interests of British North America that this continuous belt can be settled and cultivated from a few miles West of Lake of the Woods to the passes of the Rocky Mountains, and any line of communication, whether by wagon or railroad, passing through it, will eventually enjoy the great advantage of being fed by an agricultural population from one extremity to the other. No other part of the American Continent possesses an approach even to this singularly favourable disposition of soil and climate.*

"The natural resources lying within the limits of the Fertile Belt, or on its Eastern borders, are themselves of great value as local elements of future wealth and prosperity; but, in view of a communication across the continent, they acquire paramount importance. Timber, available for fuel and building purposes, coal, iron ore are widely distributed, of great purity and in considerable abundance; salt, in quantity sufficient for a dense population. All these crude elements of wealth lie within the limits or on the borders of a region of great fertility."

His Grace Archbishop Taché, of St. Boniface, whose long residence and travelled experience throughout the North-West, says :—

"The coal fields which cross the different branches of the Saskatchewan are a great source of wealth, and favor the settlement of the valley in which nature has multiplied picturesque scenery that challenges comparison with the most remarkable of its kind in the world. I can understand the exclusive attachment of the children of the Saskatchewan for their native place. Having crossed the desert, and having come to so great a distance from civilized countries, which are occasionally supposed to have a monopoly of good things, one is surprised to find in the extreme West so extensive and so beautiful a region. The Author of the universe has been pleased to spread out, by the side of the grand and wild beauties of the Rocky Mountains, the captivating pleasure grounds of the plains of the Saskatchewan "

Confining his remarks to the capabilities for stock-raising, His Grace further adds, referring to the great extent of pasturage :—

"The character and richness of its growth equalling the finest clover. It is known that in cold countries grass acquires a nutritive power which its juices have not time to develop in warmer climates."

Captain W. J. S. Pullen, R.N , comparing with other countries :—

"I have been in, viz.: Australia, America, North and South India, &c., that I have no hesitation in agreeing with Father de Smet, Mons. Borgeau, Blakiston and many others, that there is a most extensive portion of the country so long governed by the Hudson's Bay Company ready and offering a good field for colonization."

Lord Milton, who spent some time in the country, says :—

"As an agricultural country its advantages can hardly be overrated. The climate is milder than that of the same portion of Canada which lies within the same latitudes, while the soil is at least equal, if not of greater fertility. Coal of good sound quality is abundant in the Saskatchewan, Battle, Pembina and other Rivers. In some places the beds are of enormous thickness, and may be worked without sinking, as it often crops out along the river banks. Cereals of almost every description flourish even under the rude cultivation of the half-breeds. The same may be said of all the root crops which are ordinarily grown in England, Canada or the Northern States of America."

Mr. W. B Cheadle, an English gentleman who accompanied Lord Milton, also says :

"At Edmonton, eight hundred miles distant from Fort Garry, near the Western extremity, wheat grows with equal luxuriance, and yields thirty to fifty bushels to the acre, in some instances even more. The root crops I have never such equalled in England; potatoes get to an immense size, and yield enormously. Flax, hemp, tobacco, all grow well; . the cereals appear to flourish equally well; plums, strawberries, raspberries and gooseberries grow wild. The herbage of the prairie is so feeding that corn is rarely given to horses or cattle. They do their hard work, subsist entirely on grass, are most astonishingly fat; the draught oxen resemble prize animals at a cattle show. The horses we took with us were turned adrift at the beginning of winter, when snow had already fallen; they had been over-worked and were jaded and thin. In the spring we hunted them up, and found them in the finest condition, or rather too fat. The soil in La Belle Prairie, where we built our hut for the winter, was *four feet deep*, and free from rocks or gravel—the finest loam. The climate is that of Upper Canada, or perhaps rather milder. The summer is long and warm, the weather uniformly bright and fine; with the exception of occasional showers, a wet day is almost unknown. The winter is severe and unbroken by thaw, but pleasant enough to those able to house and clothe themselves warmly."

Prof. John Macoun, M.A., Botanist, who thoroughly explored the country, says :

"In Crofutt's Trans-Continental Tourists' Guide occurs the passage, speaking of the Prairie West of Antelope, on the line of the Union Pacific Railway : 'We now enter on the best grass country in the world,' and further on he says : 'The country is destined at no distant day to become the great pasture land of the continent.' "Now," says Prof. Macoun, " I have passed over these plains from Laramie to Antelope, which is represented as being the best grazing lands in the world, and which are now supporting thousands of cattle, and they bear no more comparison to our plains (the Saskatchewan) than a stubble field does to a meadow. While they have 1,000 miles of sage plains (valueless), for bunch grass soon dies out when pastured, and sage brush takes its place, we have over 1,000 miles, from East to West, of land covered at all times of the year with a thick sward of the richest grass, and which is so nutritious as to keep horses in good condition, though travelling, as ours did, at the rate of forty miles per day."

Further on he says :

"That there is a great uniformity respecting soil, humidity and temperature throughout the whole region, is apparent from the unvarying character of its natural productions. Spring flowers were found on the plains April 11th, and the frogs croaking the same evening. During 20 years in Ontario, he never observed our first spring flower (Hepatica triloba) as early as that except twice."

Again he says :

"It requires very little prophetical skill to enable any one to foretell, that very few years will elapse before this region will be teeming with flocks and herds."

The Rev. George M. Grant, in "Ocean to Ocean," says from his own experience crossing the continent as Secretary to the Engineer-in-Chief of the Canadian Pacific Railway :

"The climatological conditions are favorable for both stock raising and grain producing. The spring is as early as in Ontario, the summer is more humid, and, therefore, the grains, grasses and root crops grow better; the autumn is bright and cloudless; the very weather for harvesting; and the winter has less snow and fewer snowstorms, and, though in many parts colder, it is healthy and pleasant, because of the still dry air, the cloudless sky and bright sun. The soil is almost everywhere a peaty or sandy loam resting in clay. Its only fault is that it is too rich. Crop after crop is raised without fallow or manure."

The following extract from the Speech from the Throne of His Excellency the Lieutenant-Governor of Manitoba, at the opening of Parliament, speaking of the prosperity of the Province of Manitoba :

"A harvest was reaped of such an abundant character as to prove beyond all question that Manitoba is entitled to take the highest rank as an agricultural country."

Lord Dufferin, so highly popular as the late Governor-General of Canada, has already given in many of his able and eloquent public speeches, his opinion, as the result of his visit to the country in the ummer of 1877, pronouncing it to be one of the finest in the world.

Lastly.—Our newly-appointed Governor-General, the Marquis of Lorne, in his farewell address to the electors of Argyleshire, delivered at Inverary, thus refers to this favored portion of the Dominion :

"Some years ago, at a public meeting in Glasgow, I took the opportunity to describe the temptation offered by the Canadian Government, to men emp. ed in agriculture here, to settle in Manitoba, and since that day, as before it, hundreds of happy homesteads have risen, and the energies of the Dominion have been directed towards the construction of railways, which will make Manitoba and the North-West considerably *more accessible than is Inverary now.* Let me invite your attention to this great Province, and the vast prairies beyond. I am informed, unless one has heard or seen for himself, he can form no idea how fast the country is settling up with people from England, Scotland, Ireland, Russia. Iceland, and the older Provinces of the Dominion."

The foregoing corroborating testimony must be sufficient to carry conviction to the mind of the most ordinarily intelligent intending emigrant or investor, of the great superiority, in point of soil, climate and agricultural capacity, of this vast prairie country over that of any portion of the United States, which have arisen so rapidly from the condition of a fringe of Provinces along the Atlantic to that of a mighty nation, spreading its arms across the continent.

THE CONTRAST, IN COMPARISON WESTERN STATES.

Many readers of this pamphlet who may be intending to emigrate, and have a longing desire to realize the romance and happiness of a life in the Western States of America, drawn to that, by the glowing and attractive pictures and representations which have been held out throughout Europe, of their riches should know that Iowa and other States to-day contain thousands who would gladly leave for anywhere, if not to return to their native land, *if they could;* fever and ague, poor and unsalable land, dearly bought, have brought the inevitable end—ruin. The writer has seen too many letters telling the pitiful tale, and as a serious warning to intending emigrants and capitalists in Europe, the following is selected :

38

Editors Planters:

Dear Sirs,—A few facts from actual experience of farming in Kansas—the other side, and the truth. We have been much amused by the gushing letters of some contributors to your valuable paper, about this State, and think the actual experience of farmers like ourselves might be as valuable as the moonshine idea of men who never put a plough in the ground, or raised a calf, or wintered a Texas steer, or tried to watch a corn-field, or sell corn at 10 cents a bushel. We came here four years ago, determined to like the country. Now we believe it to be a delusion and a snare. We wanted cheap lands; we paid $1.25 per acre, but it has cost us in dead outlay, in money and in time, $5 to $20 per acre, and is all for sale less than cost.

We came to find a great stock country, where the time of feeding might be short, and cattle might live on the range all winter; we find it the worst hampered stock country we ever saw, and the grass nutritious and flesh-producing only three or four months of the year. We came to find a great wheat and corn country : we find that wheat-raisers have not averaged their seed. Corn ranges all the way from nothing to fifty bushels per acre. We expected to find a tame grass country, but so far, timothy, clover and blue grass failed, and the climate that kills wheat will kill them. We came here to find a salubrious and healthy climate ; we find it sickly, and the rates of mortality last winter along the streams terrible, so much so that we came to believe what an old doctor told us : *" That the most hardy could not expect to survive this climate fifteen years."*

We came to the "Sunny South," where the warm zephyrs ever blow : we find cattle freeze to death in every locality. We came to find a great fruit country : we find our peach trees dead to the ground. We came to find a bracing air : we have found it so that we have to brace ourselves at an angle of forty-five degrees to make headway against the wind. We came here to escape the oppression of the rich, and the high taxes : our taxes range from 2.05 to 10 per cent. on real estate, and does not pay anything. We came to find homes for the homeless, and lands for the landless : we have got homes, very poor ones, and the land we would be glad to get shut of at half price. In short, we have got the land, and it has got us in the very worst way, and every one is dissatisfied, unhappy, discouraged, and wants to get out of the country. We came to the country that was said to flow with milk and honey : we find it flowing with poverty and complaint. We find we must go where money is plenty, where labour is needed, and a market for our produce.

We live where every quarter section of land has been settled by good energetic people, who have made every effort and universally failed ; those who have done the most, and spent the most, are the most completely floored.

Such is our experience, after a fair, faithful trial of Southern Kansas. If you, Mr. Editor, can help us out in any way by advice or otherwise, you will oblige three farmers.

We have many friends East, and there are many coming West, we earnestly hope will see those few lines.

We do not wish to see our friends made paupers by doing as we have done, neither ought any more capital be wasted in this desert of a country. We can substantiate all we have subscribed our names to by more positive proof if needed, and ask that all this whole article may be published for the sake of truth.

Address,—

J. S. Calmer,
M. G. Averill,
J. T. Douglass.

The foregoing is clipped from a Kansas newspaper, and however terrible the description, bears upon its face the honest truth.

LIBERALITY OF CANADIAN LAND REGULATIONS.

The Canadian Land Regulations having been very generally represented to be more onerous and less liberal than those of the United States, it is proper to point out to intending settlers that ten dollars ($10) covers the whole of the office fees in Canada, either for a pre-emption or a homestead ; while in the Western States there are three fees, one of eight dollars, payable on entry, another of eight dollars for a commission, and another of ten dollars when the patent is issued, making twenty-six dollars ($26.00). In some of the States the fees are thirty-four dollars ($34.00). The U. S. lands are sold at $2.50 and $1.25 per acre. These prices are nearly the same, but the difference is favourable to Canada.

In fact, it is repeated that not on the Continent of America, and it is believed not elsewhere, are the Land Regulations so favourable as in Canada.

It is provided by the Canadian Naturalization Act that aliens may acquire and hold real and personal property of every description, in the same manner and in all respects as a natural born British subject.

The only disqualification of aliens is that they are not qualified to hold office under the Government or to vote at Parliamentary or municipal elections.

The oath of allegiance required of aliens who desire to become British subjects simply expresses fidelity to the Queen and Constitution, without any discrimination against the nation from which such aliens come.

To take up United States Government land, however, the following oath is required to be taken by a British subject :—

    DISTRICT COURT,
    ....Judicial District, } State of.....................
    County of......................... }

I........... ....do swear that I will support the Constitution of the United States of America, and that I do absolutely and entirely Renounce and Abjure forever all Allegiance and Fidelity to every Foreign Power, Prince, Potentate, State or Sovereignty whatever, and particularly to *Queen Victoria, of Great Britain and Ireland,* whose subject I was. And further, that I never have borne any hereditary title, or been of any of the degrees of Nobility of the country whereof I have been a subject, and that I have resided within the United States for five years last past, and in this State for one year last past.

    Subscribed and sworn to in open Court }
        this......day of............18.. } ....

    ....Clerk.

PROF. HENRY, of the Smithsonian Institute, Washington, speaking of the explorations, under the auspices of the U. S. Government, of the region between the Mississippi and the Rocky Mountains, reveals to us the startling facts :

"That the *western progress* of its population, has nearly *reached the extreme western limit* of the areas available for settlement ; and that the whole space west of the ninety-eighth parallel, embracing one-half of the entire surface of the United States, is *an arid and desolate waste*, with the exception of a narrow belt of rich land along the Pacific coast."

The importance of these official statements cannot be over-estimated in drawing public attention to our vast resources, and should not fail to carry conviction to the most obtuse intellect, that, as we have already stated, the entire expansive movement of population on the American continent will be concentrated in the direction of our fertile valleys, and the future destiny of the North-West of Canada will be a great and glorious one ; fortunate, therefore, will be descendants of those who may obtain a foothold within its gigantic borders, possessing all the true elements of future greatness and prosperity, its rapid growth will continue unparalleled.

After a careful perusal of these testimonies, on both sides, the intending emigrant must judge and decide in the future interests of himself and family, to which country he shall emigrate, the Western States or the North-West of Canada, with its home institutions and the flag of "old England."

INTERNAL COMMUNICATION.

Never lose sight of the fact that POPULATION, the sure precursor of development, and trade invariably follows the lines of railways and the course of navigable river. The settler will perceive that with such a system of rail and water communication there can never come any question of want of market. The home market, from the large influx of settlers and the immense construction of public works, will absorb nearly all the produce for years to come.

The best lands, and most advantageous situations for wood and water, are thus rapidly appropriated. The intending settler in the North-West will therefore be repaid by an attentive study of the following

RIVERS AND LAKES.

The Saskatchewan River, being the largest, is 1864 miles in length. The North and South branches rise in the Rocky Mountains within a few miles of each other. The South branch is 1092 miles in length, and the North branch 772 miles. In ascending the river from Lake Winnipeg, the Grand Rapids, 3 miles long, with 43½ feet of descent, are first reached. The character of the soil in the country drained by the Saskatchewan, is of a very superior quality. Already the country is settling up rapidly, and men of capital and experience are pushing their enterprises in that direction. Steamers sometimes run as high as Edmonton, a distance by river of about 1200 miles.

PRINCE ALBERT SETTLEMENT, on the South side of the North Saskatchewan, 45 miles below Carleton, extends a distance of about 30 miles, and numbers over 1000 settlers, who are in a highly prosperous condition. It has a steam saw and grist mill, numerous stores, &c. The distance from Winnipeg overland, is about 575 miles.

EDMONTON is the centre of a fine section of farming country, rapidly settling up with an enterprising population. The country drained by the north branch and its tributary, the *Battle River*, is considerably wooded. Edmonton is the centre of the gold washing fields of the north Saskatchewan.

BATTLEFORD, the Capital of the North-West Territory, is situate 700 miles by road west of Winnipeg, and occupies the tongue of land between the *Battle River* and the north branch of the Saskatchewan. The Canadian Pacific Railway will probably cross the river at this point, and doubtless will greatly add to the future prosperity of this ambitious young town. A fortnightly Express and Postal Service is maintained between Winnipeg, Battleford and Edmonton.

There is also direct telegraphic communication opened with Ottawa and other chief centres of the Dominion. On the branch above "the forks" of the Saskatchewan spreads the "park country," natural fields of rich land, dotted with lakes and groves. *Duck Lake*, 20 miles west, is also the nucleus of an improving colony.

Red Deer, Bow and *Belly Rivers* are tributaries of the South Saskatchewan, and drain a fine region, abounding in nutritious grasses and well adapted for stock raising.

The *Assiniboine River*, the principal tributary of *Red River*, which it joins at Winnipeg, is usually navigable as far as Fort Ellice, 213 miles from Winnipeg, by waggon road, by river about 550 miles. Its entire course is upwards af 600 miles.

The *Qu'Appelle*, the main tributary of the Assiniboine, rises near the elbow of the south branch of the Saskatchewan ; it is 250 miles long, and flows through a fine valley. The *Souris*, and the *Little Saskatchewan*, are also tributaries of the Assiniboine.

Little Saskatchewan River is a very beautiful stream, though very rapid. It drains a magnificent country, which is fast settling up, and the soil is of wonderful fertility.

Peace River is navigable for 500 miles from the Rocky Mountains, with an average depth of six feet, and drains one of the richest and most magnificent portions of the territory.

Ro ' or *Carrot River* rises in rich lands 60 miles south-west from "the forks" of the Saskatchewan, and flows through a wooded country with many lakes, generally from 30 to 50 miles south of the Saskatchewan, into which it falls after a course of 240 miles. It is estimated that there are three millions acres of land of first quality between this river and the Saskatchewan.

Swan River has a course of nearly 200 miles, running through a beautiful country, and enters Lake Winnipegoosis near its north end.

LAKES WINNIPEG, MANITOBA and WINNIPEGOOSIS are the chief lakes. Mossy Portage, four miles long, connects the head of Lake Winnipegoosis with *Cedar Lake*, on the main Saskatchewan, thus linking a line of continuous water communication 1,500 miles in length, extending from Winnipeg City to the base of the Rocky Mountains.

CONCLUSION.

We would only add, in conclusion, all intending emigrants should remember that a new country like this is not the idler's paradise, that all its mines of wealth are surrounded by bustling difficulties. It also has its drawbacks ; no country is quite perfect or without them. Its great superiority is, that it is a land of opportunities. Its rapid growth and present prosperity may be attributed to three principal causes, viz.: First, its salubrity of climate ; second, the extraordinary fertility and adaptibility of its soil ; and third, to the liberal homstead law in force under the provisions of the Dominion Lands Act.

Prof. Macoun, the eminent Canadian Botanist and Explorer, on his return in November last from an official tour throughout a great portion of the North-West, in an instructive lecture delivered before a large audience in Winnipeg, said, "that he, who had seen more of the North-West than any man in Canada, was surprised to find places that had *existence last spring*, had now regular mails, weekly or more frequent, and post offices were established where *five months ago there were no houses.*" From this, those interested in Great Britain will be able to form some idea of the rapid development of the country, and it is at least food for honest pride that Canadian enterprise is so actively spreading civilization over this land of promise as to cause even the astonishment of our fast go-ahead American cousins across the border. It is to be a first-class new world power, with its Danube of the Saskatchewan, and its Baltic and Black Sea of Lake Winnipeg and Lake Superior. A broad field of commercial activity is now open before us, and the hundreds of thousands who will be attracted hither will enter into triumphant competition with the agriculture of the world in its central marts. Finally, we repeat, here, as in no other portion of this continent, are *openings* to-day that yield their wealth to brains, energy, pluck, whether with or without capital, more than is actually necessary to start with fairly ; and if a man wants to work honestly for what he has, he can do it as well here as in any land beneath the sun. In a few short years our yet undeveloped wealth will astonish the world, when our coal and iron mines are laid bare, when our vast plains and hills are covered with flocks and herds, when our valleys supply grain to Europe and the East, and the great Canadian Pacific Railway links England, Canada, Japan and China in one great belt of commerce and mutual prosperity.

DOMINION LANDS REGULATIONS.

The following Regulations for the sale and settlement of Dominion Lands in the Province of Manitoba and the North-West Territories shall, on and after the first day of January, 1882, be substituted for the Regulations now in force, bearing date the 25th day of May last :

1. The surveyed lands in Manitoba and the North-West Territories shall, for the purpose of these Regulations, be classified as follows :

CLASS A.—Lands within twenty-four miles of the main line or any branch line of the Canadian Pacific Railway, on either side thereof.

CLASS B.—Lands within twelve miles, on either side, of any projected line of railway (other than the Canadian Pacific Railway) published in the *Canada Gazette.*

CLASS C.—Lands south of the main line of the Canadian Pacific Railway not included in Class A or B.

CLASS D.—Lands other than those in Classes A, B and C.

2. The even-numbered sections in all the foregoing classes are to be held exclusively for homesteads and pre-emptions.

a. Except in Class D, where they may be affected by colonization agreements, as hereinafter provided.

b. Except where it may be necessary out of them to provide wood lots for settlers.

c. Except in cases where the Minister of the Interior, under provisions of the Dominion Lands Act, may deem it expedient to withdraw certain lands, and sell them at public auction or otherwise deal with them as the Governor-in-Council may direct.

3. The odd-numbered sections in Class A are reserved for the Canadian Pacific Railway.

4. The odd numbered sections in Classes B and C shall be for sale at $2.50 per acre, payable at the time of sale.

a. Except where they have been or may be dealt with otherwise by the Governor-in-Council.

5. The odd-numbered sections in Class D shall be for sale at $2 per acre, payable at time of sale.

a. Except where they have been or may be dealt with otherwise by the Governor-in-Council.

b. Except lands affected by colonization agreement, as hereinafter provided.

6. Persons who, subsequent to survey, but before the issue of the Order-in-Council of 9th October, 1879, excluding odd-numbered sections from homestead entry, took possession of land in odd-numbered sections by residing on and cultivating the same, shall, if continuing so to occupy them, be permitted to obtain homestead and pre-emption entries as if they were on even-numbered sections.

PRE-EMPTIONS.

7. The prices for pre-emption lots shall be as follows :—

For lands in Classes A, B and C, $2.50 per acre.
For lands in Class D, $2.00 per acre.

Payments shall be made in one sum at the end of three years from the date of entry, or at such earlier date as a settler may, under the provisions of the Dominion Lands Act, obtain a patent for the homestead to which such pre-emption lot belongs.

COLONIZATION.

Plan No. 1.

8. Agreements may be entered into with any company or persons (hereinafter called the party) to colonize and settle tracts of land on the following conditions :

a. The party applying must satisfy the Government of its good faith and ability to fulfil the stipulations contained in these regulations.

b. The tract of land granted to any party shall be in Class D.

9. The odd-numbered section within such tract may be sold to the party at $2 per acre, payable, one-fifth in cash at the time of entering into the contract, and the balance in four equal annual instalments from and after that time. The party shall also pay to the Government five cents per acre for the survey of the land purchased by it, the same to be payable in four equal annual instalments at the same time as the instalments of the purchase money. Interest at the rate of six per cent. per annum shall be charged on all past due instalments.

a. The party shall, within five years from the date of the contract, colonize its tract.

b. Such colonization shall consist in placing two settlers on homesteads on each even-numbered section, and also two settlers on each odd-numbered section.

c. The party may be secured for advances made to settlers on homesteads according to the provisions of the 10th section of the Act 44 Victoria, chap. 16. (The Act passed in 1881 to amend the Dominion Lands Acts.)

d. The homestead of 160 acres shall be the property of the settler, and he shall have the right to purchase the pre-emption lot belonging to his homestead at $2 per acre, payable in one sum at the end of three years from the date of entry, or at such earlier date as he may, under the provisions of the Dominion Lands Act, obtain a patent for his homestead.

e. When the settler on a homestead does not take entry for the pre-emption lot to which he has a right, the party may within three months after the settler's right has elapsed purchase the same at $2 per acre, payable in cash at the time of purchase.

10. In consideration of having colonized its tract of land in the manner set forth in sub-section b of the last preceding clause, the party shall be allowed a rebate of one-half of the original purchase-money of the odd-numbered sections in its tract.

a. During each of the five years covered by the contract an enumeration shall be made of the settlers placed by the party in its tract, in accordance with sub-section b of clause 9 of these regulations, and for each bonâ fide settler so found therein a rebate of one hundred and twenty dollars shall be credited to the party ; but the sums so credited shall not, in the aggregate, at any time exceed one hundred and twenty dollars for each bonâ fide settler found within the tract, in accordance with said sub-section, at the time of latest enumeration.

b. On the expiration of the five years an enumeration shall be made of the bonâ fide settlers on the tract, and if they are found to be as many in number and placed in the manner stipulated for in sub-section b of clause 9 of these regulations, a further and final rebate of forty dollars per settler shall be credited to the party, which sum, when added to those previously credited, will amount to one-half of the purchase money of the odd-numbered sections and reduce the price thereon to one dollar per acre. But if it should be found that the full number of settlers required by these regulations are not on the tract, or are not placed in conformity with the said sub-section *b*, of clause 9 of these regulations, then, for each settler fewer than the required number, or not placed in conformity with the said sub-sections, the party shall forfeit one hundred and sixty dollars of rebate.

c. If at any time during the existence of the contract the party shall have failed to perform any of the conditions thereof, the Governor-in-Council may cancel the sale of the land purchased by it and deal with the party as may seem meet under the circumstances.

d. To be entitled to rebate, the party shall furnish to the Minister of the Interior evidence that will satisfy him that the tract has been colonized and settled in accordance with sub-section *b* of clause 9 of these regulations.

PLAN NUMBER TWO.

11. To encourage settlement by capitalists who may desire to cultivate larger farms than can be purchased where the regulations provide that two settlers shall be placed on each section, agreements may be entered into with any company or person (hereinafter called the party) to colonize and settle tracts of land on the following conditions :

a. The party applying must satisfy the Government of its good faith and ability to fulfil the stipulations contained in these regulations.

b. The tract of land granted to any party shall be in Class D.

c. All the land within the tract may be sold to the party at two dollars per acre, payable in cash at the time of entering into the contract. The party shall, at the same time, pay to the Government five cents per acre for the survey of the land purchased by it.

d. The party shall, within five years from the date of the contract, colonize the township or townships comprised within its tract.

e. Such colonization shall consist in placing one hundred and twenty-eight *bona fide* settlers within each township.

12. In consideration of having colonized its tract of land in the manner set forth in sub-section *e* of the last preceding clause, the party shall be allowed a rebate of one-half of the original purchase money of its tract.

a. During each of the five years covered by the contract an enumeration shall be made of the settlers placed by the party in its tract, and, for each *bona fide* settler so found therein, a rebate of one hundred and twenty dollars shall be repaid to the party ; but the sums so repaid shall not, in the aggregate, at any time exceed one hundred and twenty dollars for each *bona fide* settler found within the tract, in accordance with the said sub-section at the time of the latest enumeration.

b. On the expiration of the five years an enumeration shall be made of the *bona fide* settlers placed by the party in its tract, and if they are found to be as many in number and placed in the manner stipulated for in sub-section *e* of clause 11 of these regulations, a further and final rebate of forty dollars per settler shall be repaid, which sum, when added to those previously repaid to the party, will amount to one-half of the purchase money of its tract and reduce the price thereof to one dollar per acre. But if it should be found that the full number of settlers required by these regulations are not on the tract, or are not placed in conformity with the said sub-section, then, for each settler fewer than the required number or not settled in conformity with the said sub-section, the party shall forfeit one hundred and sixty dollars of rebate.

c. To be entitled to rebate, the party shall furnish to the Minister of the Interior evidence that will satisfy him that the tract has been colonized and settled in accordance with sub-section *e* of clause 11 of these regulations.

OFFICIAL NOTICE.

13. The Government shall give notice in the *Canada Gazette* of all agreements entered into for the colonization and settlement of tracts of land under the foregoing plans, in order that the public may respect the rights of the purchasers.

TIMBER FOR SETTLERS.

14. The Minister of the Interior may direct the reservation of any odd or even numbered section having timber upon it, to provide wood for homestead settlers on sections without it ; and each such settler may, where the opportunity for so doing exist, purchase a wood lot, not exceeding 20 acres, at the price of $5 per acre in cash.

15. The Minister of the Interior may grant under the provisions of the Dominion Land Acts, license to cut timber on lands within surveyed townships. The lands covered with such license are thereby withdrawn from homestead and pre-emption entry and from sale.

PASTURAGE LANDS.

16. Under the authority of the Act 44 Victoria, Chap. 16, leases of tracts for grazing purposes may be granted on the following conditions :

a. Such leases to be for a period of not exceeding twenty-one years, and no single lease shall cover a greater area than 100,000 acres.

b. In surveyed territory, the land embraced by the lease shall be described in townships and sections. In unsurveyed territory the party to whom a lease is promised shall, before the issue of the lease, cause a survey of the tract to be made, at his own expense, by a Dominion Land Surveyor, under instructions from the Surveyor-General ; and the plan and field notes of such survey shall be deposited on record in the Department of the Interior.

c. The lessee shall pay an annual rental at the rate of $10 for every 1,000 acres embraced by his lease, and shall, within three years from the granting of the lease, place on the tract one head of cattle for every ten acres of land embraced by the lease, and shall during its term maintain cattle thereon in at least that proportion.

d. After placing the prescribed number of cattle upon the tract leased, the lessee may purchase land within his leasehold for a home farm and *corral*, paying therefor $2.00 per acre in cash.

e. Failure to fulfil any of the conditions of his lease shall subject the lessee to forfeiture thereof.

17. When two or more parties apply for a grazing lease of the same land tenders shall be invited, and the lease shall be granted to the party offering the highest premium therefor in addition to the rental. The said premium to be paid before the issue of the lease.

GENERAL PROVISIONS.

18. Payments for land may be in cash, scrip, or Police or Military Bounty Warrants.

19. These regulations shall not apply to lands valuable for town plots, or to coal or other mineral lands, or to stone or marble quarries, or to lands having water power thereon; or to sections 11 and 29 in each Township, which are school Lands, or Sections 8 and 26, which belong to the Hudson's Bay Company.

By order,

LINDSAY RUSSELL,
Surveyor General.

DEPARTMENT OF THE INTERIOR,
Ottawa, 23rd December, 1881.